Lilith Circle Guide

A Small Group Study
by Monette Chilson

Based on the Girl God Anthology
Original Resistance: Reclaiming Lilith, Reclaiming Ourselves

©2021 Girl God Books

ISBN: 978-82-93725-15-2

www.thegirlgod.com

Girl God Books

Original Resistance: Reclaiming Lilith, Reclaiming Ourselves
There is, perhaps, no more powerful archetype of female resistance than Lilith. As women across the globe rise up against the patriarchy, Lilith stands beside them, misogyny's original challenger. This anthology—a chorus of voices hitting chords of defiance, liberation, anger and joy—reclaims the goodness of women bold enough to hold tight to their essence. Through poetry, prose, incantation, prayer and imagery, women from all walks of life invite you to join them in the revolutionary act of claiming their place—of reclaiming themselves.

Re-visioning Medusa: from Monster to Divine Wisdom
A remarkable collection of essays, poems, and art by scholars who have researched Her, artists who have envisioned Her, and women who have known Her in their personal story. All have spoken with Her and share something of their communion in this anthology.

Willendorf's Legacy: The Sacred Body
Travel through time and discover a world where the fullness of women was both admired and deified. Reclaim your beautiful Goddess body through the rich pages of this powerful collection of art, poetry and essays celebrating our divine inheritance as daughters of Willendorf.

New Love: a reprogramming toolbox for undoing the knots
A powerful combination of emotional/spiritual techniques, art and inspiring words for women who wish to move away from patriarchal thought. *New Love* includes a mixture of compelling thoughts and suggestions for each day, along with a "toolbox" to help you change the parts of your life you want to heal.

A Deeper Wisdom: The 12 Steps from a Woman's Perspective
A Deeper Wisdom is for all women whether or not they've ever set foot in a recovery meeting. We've all wrestled with habits of thought and behavior that did not support the life we wanted. ADW's life-practice transforms self-criticism into self-compassion and the suffering that fuels habit-energy into joy.

The Girl God
A book for children young and old, celebrating the Divine Female by Trista Hendren. Magically illustrated by Elisabeth Slettnes with quotes from various faith traditions and feminist thinkers.

My Name is Lilith
Whether you are familiar with the legend of Lilith or hearing it for the first time, you will be carried away by this lavishly illustrated tale of the world's first woman. This creative retelling of Lilith's role in humanity's origins will empower girls and boys to seek relationships based on equality rather than hierarchy.

Complete list of Girl God publications at www.thegirlgod.com

NOTE FROM THE PUBLISHER:

We first compiled these voices—a chorus of made up of women from around the world—in *Original Resistance: Reclaiming Lilith, Reclaiming Ourselves*—the anthology we released in 2019. This guide is a companion to that book, and you will need a copy of *Original Resistance* to lead a Lilith Circle.

You may choose to have one copy which you pass around at your circle gatherings, or each woman may want her own copy, particularly if you are meeting virtually. If you decide to place an order of ten or more copies for your group, we will offer a 10% discount and include one complimentary copy of *My Name is Lilith*, our gorgeously illustrated picture book.

For almost a decade, Girl God Books has been publishing books that usher the feminine divine—in Her many splendored forms—into the world. With the 2019 publication of *Original Resistance: Reclaiming Lilith, Reclaiming Ourselves*, we developed a curriculum that Monette has rolled out selectively in small intimate groups. Participants have experienced profound shifts in the way they are able to access the feminine divine within them in new and powerful ways. Working with women in person and seeing women utilize the material online during our beta launch, we have witnessed the power of taking our words off the page and into your lives.

Now, for the first time ever, we are bringing this work to women all over the world through our *Lessons in Lineage* virtual learning community.

Lessons in Lineage will help you awaken what you were likely never given. And not in an abstract way. We will look into the faces of women and experience the divine through bodies that bleed like ours. We will encounter the Goddesses who have been lost to us. We will see ourselves reflected in them and we will heal together.

Through virtual circles, we will rebuild our inner knowing by filling each other up with the faces of the divine feminine. We will dive deep into the Goddesses that few have dared to speak of, much less honor, for millennia. We will learn about them, but then we will explore them, breathing them in, making them our own.

If you are ready to expand your inner world to match your dreams, come sit with us. In our virtual circles, we will reclaim Mother God in all Her many forms.

We would like to invite you to explore *Lessons in Lineage*, a comprehensive curriculum of the lost legacy of the feminine divine at <u>www.thegirlgod.com/lessons_in_lineage</u>.

TABLE OF CONTENTS

INTRODUCTION: LILITH WAS THE FIRST, BUT LET HER NOT BE THE LAST

There is much talk these days about the rise of the feminine and how it will heal us and our world. Often, however, we picture this cataclysmic shift in humanity within the patriarchal worldview, as if the feminine way will simply be a kinder, gentler version of the masculine.

But it is not a different version of reality, it is a new one entirely. One that values differently and processes differently. A way that can be used by both men and women.

To get there, we cannot read a manual or examine a flowchart or analyze the data or even find the "best" woman to lead us there.

Because, my friends, the best woman for the job is you. And me. And every single one of us.

We are not building a hierarchy to take us there—we are joining hands to form a circle which expands each time a woman awakens to the call within her.

As I write this introduction Kamala Harris is being sworn in as the first female Vice President of the United States. She is leading us in the expansion of our circle at this crucial moment in history. As her mother told her when she was a child, "You may be the first, Kamala, but make sure you are not the last." In other words, keep growing the circle of female leaders who are writing a different storyline for women by the way they live their lives.

This book will point you to your circle and provide the resources you'll need to birth many new storylines alongside them. You may already have a group of women in mind to join you in this work. Or maybe not. Maybe the work is calling to you and the right companions will appear.

Either way, buckle up because we are going to turn ancient myths about femininity and what it means to be a woman on their head! Not with logic, reason and factual "proof," but with stories that have been hidden from us even as their echoes coursed through our veins.

At long last, we will reconcile our inner knowing with the narrative that mirrors it rather than denying and subverting it.

We will fully embody our sacred feminine nature through the power of storytelling, specifically through the story of the world's first woman as conceptualized by Western civilizations.

Our compass for this journey is not historical data. Nor is it archaeological artifacts. Not even newly discovered scrolls with words that confirm our knowing.

Our compass is an artistic compilation of women's encounters with Lilith. Some are grounded in research; some in lived experience; some in poetry; and others painted and sung. All were birthed by trusting the inner voice we've been conditioned to ignore.

The voice that knows something is right for her or wrong for her. The voice that leads you along a path that is yours alone to walk.

Lilith may have been the first woman to subvert the expectations of her—but let her not be the last.

WELCOME:

First of all, welcome to this circle and to the larger global collective of Lilith Circles. You can connect with other women doing this work in our Original Resistance Facebook group, which you can find linked at the top of the Girl God Books Facebook page.

Reading this collection of writings on the critical female archetype of Lilith is powerful in and of itself. Working through the content communally creates exactly the kind of soul connection we need during this time of feminine rising. So, thank you for heeding the call.

It is my hope that this study guide will support your group, giving you the structure you need to do this transformative work, while leaving ample room for you to customize and alter as needed. Please consider this a jumping off point and feel free to chart your own course through this rediscovery that is, by its archetypal nature, both extremely personal and universal. I believe that the very act of doing this work together will bond you, forming the kind of close-knit unit Abby Wambach describes in her book *Wolf Pack*—one that supports its members as they change their inner and outer landscapes.

The curriculum is broken up into three broad sections—Rediscovering Lilith, Reclaiming Lilith and Reclaiming Ourselves. Each of these parts is further broken down into three sessions, for a total of nine group meetings. I recommend a weekly Lilith Circle; however, meetings can be weekly, monthly or even condensed to fit into a retreat format where a group could cover one or two sessions per day over a long weekend or week-long intensive.

To get the most out of this guide, I recommend that you read the anthology in its entirety first— front to back. Then, revisit the passages before each circle and discuss with the group.

Each session will follow the same structure, giving your time together, a rhythm that will become predictable, allowing you to focus your energy on the work, rather than its organization. The core work of the group will be done through reading, writing and sharing within a sacred circle of trust.

Finally, I encourage you to set guiding principles for your group that will create an atmosphere in which each voice is valued and confidentiality is assured. I am including two examples from group leaders I admire. Interestingly, these two women are both part of my own wolf pack, and I encourage you to explore their work. They have graciously granted us permission to use these graphics in your groups. You can find the graphics in the tools section of the Lilith Circle tab: http://thegirlgod.com/lilith_circle.php.

Feel free to adopt one or both or to create your own visual to suit your group. I suggest reviewing these during the opening of every meeting. They are the bedrock on which your group and the individuals in it will grow.

    Listen with your heart.
    Observe your own biases.
    Venture into unfamiliar territory.
    Expect the best.

    Love first. Always.

    Courtesy of Tracie Jae (www.quietrebellife.com)

Basic Circle Agreements:

Confidentiality and Safety
No one is broken. Please no fixing.
Be present and hold space of love, honor and respect.
Communicate.
Please no selling.

Courtesy of Debra Graugnard (www.joyfullylivingwellness.com)

Also….

Don't forget to think through the logistics of your group before you start. You'll need to decide how many people you'd like to have. Establish a range—I suggest a minimum of four or five and maximum of 10 or 12. Pick a place. Or do it virtually, as is still advisable as of this writing.

If in person, you can keep it simple and have a consistent location or mix it up and rotate between members' homes. If you want a more formal setting with everyone around a big table, consider booking a room at a local library or community center. Want it to be more relaxed? Sit around on couches or pillows at someone's home.

What date/time will work best for your prospective members? Are your members in different locations? If so, make a plan that works across the time zones. Choose a video meeting platform like Zoom that works for your members. Decide on your schedule including the length of meetings. You'll need a minimum of one hour and probably don't want to ask people to commit to more than a two-hour block. Do you want to have a simple snack at meetings? Bring one to the first meeting and have a sign-up sheet so others can pitch in for future gatherings.

I look forward to hearing what you learn and how you make this material your own. Please drop me a note with questions, comments or feedback (monette@monettechilson.com). I am here to support you however I can.

GROUP STUDY MISSION

This small group guide is designed to help women communally process the archetypal awakenings they may experience while reading *Original Resistance: Reclaiming Lilith, Reclaiming Ourselves*. Through reading aloud, journaling and sharing, women will create a safe place to explore the implications of adapting a new paradigm of femininity inspired by Lilith.

WHAT TO EXPECT

Facilitators: Your role as the leader of this group is simply to create a container for growth and to hold space for those who join you on this journey. Let go of any sense of responsibility for the outcome. Be very clear that your role is to offer opportunities for growth. It is up to each person how they choose to avail themselves of the opportunities offered.

With that said, be open to where this study takes you and your group. It is not a study with a specific pre-planned result because we are not wired for such prescribed outcomes.

Participants: Consider the path that led you here. I bet there were synchronicities and "coincidences" that conspired to encourage your participation in this circle. I am so very glad you did not dismiss them and chose to follow them here.

For all of us, this process will be a bit like rewiring our operating systems. It turns out that critical feminine input was missing from the narrative upon which our DNA was built. Our ancestors only heard tales of the hero's journey and were deprived of the heroine's. Over campfires, war stories became lore and then became the bedrock of civilization. Women's triumphs went unheeded which told us they were not worth noting. We built a history upon this, and it was truly *his* story. *Her* story has been neglected from the dawn of time.

Consider this a new dawn—the dawning of the sacred feminine in you and for you. For nine weeks, we are banding together and committing ourselves to acknowledging all that's been lost and beginning the process of rebuilding herstory which, it turns out, is *our* story.

MAP FOR THE JOURNEY

We will work our way from outer to inner knowledge, beginning by wrapping ourselves up in the rich cocoon of Lilith's story; moving into claiming her as our spiritual ancestor; and, finally, claiming her sovereignty for ourselves.

Following is a map for this journey, outlining each of these three parts of our work and the three sessions contained within each of them. The readings covered in each session are included for your reference. Remember, we encourage you to read the entire anthology before you begin your circle and to revisit the current session's readings before each circle. It is my experience that I hear something different each time I read them. You will hear what you need to hear whether it is your first reading or your fiftieth. I even get new messages when I reread the pieces that I wrote!

Just a reminder that this is the companion guide to the anthology *Original Resistance: Reclaiming Lilith, Reclaiming Ourselves*. You will need at least one copy for your group to share as the readings referenced are taken from that book and are not reprinted in this guide. Ideally, each member will have a copy of the book (either in printed or digital form), so that they can spend time with the readings outside of the group work. There is an inexpensive PDF version available for those who are on a tight budget. You can find it at: http://thegirlgod.com/sale1.php.

You will notice that some of the items in the "suggested readings" section in each session are not readings at all, but images from the anthology. Because images speak to us in different ways that language does, these artistic expressions are important. Please don't skip them!

I suggest facilitators use their "share screen" functionality to let the group absorb the images together. If this is not possible each person can look at the images in their copy of the anthology. Don't rush through this with a glance. Spend about a minute on each image.

PART ONE: REDISCOVERING LILITH

This first section—Rediscovering Lilith—is not the time for figuring out the facts of Lilith's existence. Try not to cast doubt on the power of this story by asking, "Is it true?"

It is a time to meet her with a curious shake of the hand and a welcoming, "Nice to meet you!" To marvel at her self-knowing and her bravery. A full-body embrace of her is not our work in these first few sessions. That will come later.

SESSION 1: Who is Lilith?

SESSION 2: How has Lilith been distorted and suppressed?

SESSION 3: What does Lilith stir or reawaken in you?

The Deep Within by Lucy Pierce (p. 121) IMAGE

Lilith's Song (Fly Away) by Vicki Scotti (p. 150)

Lilith as Sexual Liberator by Joey Morris (pp. 40-47)

Outraged Ancestral Mother Prayer by Molly Remer (p. 205-206)

PART TWO: RECLAIMING LILITH

Now that we have made Lilith's acquaintance; delved a bit into how distortions and suppressions might have kept us from meeting her sooner; and felt the initial stirrings of her presence, we are ready to reclaim her as an archetype, Goddess, spiritual guide or soul sister—whichever conceptualization rings truest to you. This is our time to explore the meaning of Lilith more deeply. This is the inquisitive stage where we determine who Lilith is to us and began to see how reclaiming her may shift our understanding of the definition of the feminine and the divine.

SESSION 4: What does Lilith have to teach us about feminine strength?

Hymn to Lilith by Nuit Moore (p. 84)

No Turning Back by Birgit Langhammer (pp. 38-39)

Goddess #5 by Birgit Langhammer (p. 37) IMAGE

Hear Lilith by Patricia Campagna (pp. 48-49)

Lilith Rising by Arlene Bailey (p. 116) IMAGE

Lilith—Sacred Sovereignty of the Womanspirit by Nuit Moore (pp. 146-149)

Daughters of Lilith Can Be Muslim Too by Riem Farahat (pp. 50-56)

Ode to Lilith by Joyce McCauley-Benner (p. 143)

SESSION 5: Do I have to choose between Lilith and Eve?

Lilith Eve, a Child and a Woman for our Tomorrows by Lizette Galima Tapia-Raquel (pp. 88-89)

Eve by Lucy Pierce (pp. 102-105)

Painting from *The Song of Lilith* by Liliana Kleiner, Ph.D. (p. 18) IMAGE

Daughter of Lilith by Tamara Albanna (pp. 99-100)

Garden of Eden by Asia Morgenthaler (p. 57) IMAGE

Lilith & Eve by Luisah Teish (pp. 133-142)

SESSION 6: How does Lilith's story affect my self-image and my creator image?

Reclaiming Our Time: Why Women Must Uncover Our Ancient History by Christena Cleveland, Ph.D. (pp. 5-8)

Lilith and the Black Madonna by Susan Scott (p. 188-190)

Lilith Stained Glass Window by Breanna Bowling (p. 83) IMAGE

The Hag's Prayer, Hissed from Crone to Innocent by Danielle Dulsky (p. 199-200)

Wind Dancer Wind by Elisabeth Slettnes (p. 207) IMAGE

The Dark Goddess in the Sky by Nicole Fair (pp. 106-110)

Shamelessly Naked by Donna Snyder (p. 132)

PART THREE: RECLAIMING OURSELVES

This final section of our study will help us integrate what we've learned about Lilith and about her significance as an archetype. These last three sessions are crucial because they ensure what we have intuited about ourselves during our time together is not left behind. This is where our knowledge coalesces with our knowing and begins to guide us.

SESSION 7: Can we embrace parts of ourselves we've rejected as "unfeminine?"

The Outraged Ancestral Mother by Molly Remer (pp. 202-204)

Reclaim Lilith and BE the Original Resistance by Hazel DeHealer (pp. 85-86)

The Wound by Lucy Pierce (p. 101) IMAGE

Lilith Speaks by Molly Remer (p. 98)

The Song of Lilith II by Liliana Kleiner, Ph.D. (p. 183) IMAGE

Lessons from the Dark Mother by Jaclyn Cherie (pp. 125-131)

Ashes and Spark by K.A. Laity (p. 22)

SESSION 8: What does Lilith model that I want more of in my life?

And I Rise by Arlene Bailey (p. 117)

Lilith Rising by Arlene Bailey (p. 116) IMAGE

SESSION 9: What is one tangible action that Lilith has inspired me to take in my life?

THE COMPLETE CURRICULUM:

The last section was your map, and this one is your guidebook. You may want to mark your place as you progress through this curriculum. Each of your nine sessions is outlined in detail, allowing you to implement the curriculum with little or no preparation. Simply open to your bookmark and let Lilith lead you.

The Coming of Lilith by Arlene Bailey

PART ONE—REDISCOVERING LILITH

Have you ever met someone and had that feeling that you'd met before? In a past life perhaps? Or in an alternate reality? Maybe just that *deja vu* sense that you've met before. That is what meeting Lilith may be like for you. She is someone whose genetic code is already within us, but who has been lost to us.

The best analogy I can think of is a closed adoption where the identity of the person who gave you life is sealed away and systemically kept from you. We are going to remedy that in this first part of our time together. We will unseal the envelops where your feminine heritage has been stashed away (session one); we will hold it up to the light and compare it to the story we'd been told about women's origins and nature (session two); and we will sit and listen to what this new knowledge stirs and awakens within us (session three).

We have included journaling pages—but feel free to also utilize the blank spaces within for doodling or additional notes. Lilith was not one to stay inside the lines—so take her bold example and take up space in this workbook!

Painting from *The Song of Lilith* by Liliana Kleiner, Ph.D.

Session 1: WHO IS LILITH?

INTRODUCTION TO GROUP FORMAT & TO EACH OTHER

Leader: Discuss your impetus for starting the group and vision for it. Finish with your personal introduction.

Participants: Introduce yourselves, focusing on "being" rather than "doing" descriptors—who you are at your essence rather than a role (mom, wife, sister) or a job (teacher, lawyer, plumber), including your passions and reasons for interest in the group. Set time limit to help keep the session on track (3 minutes +/- depending on group size and session length).

GROUP TENETS:

This is where you remind your group of the environment you are creating—one that is safe, confidential and loving. One where we all get to participate at a level that is comfortable for us. No one person or person should monopolize the group's time. You may choose to remind members that we are here to support, not fix, one another. Remember, you can choose to use one of the graphics from our introduction or create your own to visually convey your group's tenets.

You can also provide logistical guidance here—silence cellphones, snack availability and restroom directions if in person; muting when not speaking, chat availability and procedures for sharing if on Zoom. I find it easier to simply have the person who wants to speak unmute and do so, though you can also suggest the hand raising function.

OPENING NOTES:

Remember, we are not here to discern *the* truth, but *our* truth. We will be working with an ancient myth that holds different truths for us all. Try not to get too hung up on the "facts." They are your mind's distraction from the real work of extracting truth that will transform you. Soak in this perspective offered by Joseph Campbell who has made mythology his life's work:

"Mythology is not a lie, mythology is poetry, it is metaphorical. It has been well said that mythology is the penultimate truth—penultimate because the ultimate cannot be put into words. It is beyond words. Beyond images, beyond that bounding rim of the Buddhist Wheel of Becoming. Mythology pitches the mind beyond that rim, to what can be known but not told."
—Joseph Campbell, *The Power of Myth*

INTRODUCTORY READING: *My Name is Lilith* by Monette Chilson / illustrated by Arna Baartz

This gorgeously illustrated picture book on Lilith is FREE with your group's purchase of 10+ copies of *Original Resistance*. This book, written for children but inspiring to all, can be read in less than 15 minutes, and will introduce your group to Lilith via story and imagery. You may screen share the book with your group during the reading. We have included the words on the following pages for those who may not have the book.

My Name is Lilith by Monette Chilson

You may think I'm a stranger, but—truth be known—we met long ago, when you were still in a cradle. I came to you and tenderly rocked you, singing lullabies to calm your soul so new to this earthly realm.

I wish I could tell you only loving things about our time together. While I brought only kind-hearted intentions to you, the world saw something else. They were afraid of me.

They hung amulets to ward me off and recited in fear, "Lilith abi"—"Go away, Lilith." Try saying it out loud. Lilith abi sounds a lot like lullaby, doesn't it?

You might think I did something very bad to cause such fear. I don't like gossip, so I will tell you the story myself and let you make up your own mind.

Most people believe that the first woman on Earth was Eve. But what if she wasn't? What if I told you there was one here before her? How do I know this? Because that woman was me.

Once upon a time, I lived in the most beautiful garden. Perhaps you have heard of it? It was called Eden, which means paradise. And it was that, at least in the beginning.

It was filled with the most exotic plants and fantastical array of animals that lived peacefully with each other and with us. Yes, us. For I was not alone. I was with Adam.

Are you feeling skeptical, wondering why you have heard only of Eve, but never of me? I don't blame you. Those who came after me did quite a good job of erasing all traces of me. And what they couldn't erase, they twisted into the darkest kind of evil. It is time for me to shed some light on that darkness. And that's where we will start—with the light.

If you've read stories from the Bible, you might remember a line near the beginning where God says, "Let there be light!" Then the story goes on to tell how God made the heavens and the earth; the water and the land; the plants and the animals; and the people—men and women.

But if you look closely, you'll see there are two different versions of the story. In the first one, man and woman are created together from the same earth. That woman was me. In the second one woman is created after man from one of his ribs. That woman was Eve.

Eve was my replacement after I fled the garden. "But why would you leave paradise?" you might ask. The truth is that I left because by staying I would surely have lost myself. Let me explain. God gave us only a few simple instructions—have children to populate our sanctuary; take care of all the plants and animals; and eat the fruit for our nourishment and delight.

There was no divine edict elevating one of us above the other, but Adam began acting as though he were in charge. He called me a helpmate, and my skin prickled. He said it with such kindness, though, that I ignored my body's knowing response.

We both had so many ideas about how to care for our garden home, but I soon tired of helping carry out his plans, while he deemed mine impractical. I didn't understand why we couldn't be the joint heirs of the garden God proclaimed us to be.

Surely, there was more than enough work for us to do side-by-side, more than enough divine inspiration to go around. I kept hearing God's words in my head, "In my image I create you—

male and female, I create you." They were spoken in a parental voice that carried both mother and father within it.

I knew that I would not be able to mirror God's goodness if I stayed in that place. Outwardly, I was in paradise. Inwardly, I could feel Adam's desire to control me through his love-cloaked words. I didn't want someone constantly trying to do what was best for me. I wanted a partner—an equal—who would live life with me.

Maybe God knew this was coming, for I don't think much of what happens surprises God. In any case, God had given me a special word that only I knew and called it ineffable, which means it was too sacred to speak. God gave it to me in a dream, and I knew I was only to use it if my life depended on it. One day I woke up and knew it did, for the truest part of me was dying.

Sometimes people think that being surrounded by beautiful things—wearing fancy clothes and living in lavish style—seeps in and makes them happy inside. Let me assure you, it does not. My surroundings could not have been more ideal, yet inside, my soul was crying out.

I won't lie. A tear trickled down my cheek when I suddenly knew this was the end of my time in the garden. I would not miss Adam's dismissiveness, but I was sad because I was afraid I'd let God down. That the plan for men and women to live in harmony with plants and animals would be ruined once I left.

Soon enough I realized that I was not powerful enough to ruin God's plan. If humanity was not yet ready for living in harmony, God would find another way until people were ready. God is patient. If they needed to live in hierarchy, rather than harmony, for a while, so be it.

And with that, I uttered the unutterable—still not quite sure if I said it out loud or simply as a silent offering to God—and was whisked away from the garden as if by magic. For when God works, it often feels like magic.

Life outside of paradise was not as bad as you might think. In some ways it was a relief to be free of another's expectations of me. I was no longer tormented by the many ways I fell short of Adam's idea of a perfect woman.

Once I left the make-believe perfection of the garden behind, I was finally able to figure out who I really was. I was able to just be Lilith. Not the mother of the human race. Not the wife of the first man. Not the prototype for all the females who would follow.

Just Lilith.

I felt free. Free to experience all that being human entails. And I didn't feel banished by God. I felt like I carried a divine spark inside me. And it felt like God put it there—a parting gift to make our physical separation more bearable. God became more of an indwelling—what some call Shekinah, breath of God.

Are you wondering what I did to frighten people so? Well, once I left the garden, I left behind my opportunity for motherhood. Some days this didn't bother me much, but other days, I pined for a child of my own.

I would sneak as close as I could to newborn infants, inhaling their scent and singing soothing songs to them. I never harmed them, but people feared I would. You see, I had a special affinity for these new souls, bound as we were by the shock of acclimating to life outside of paradise. They, fresh from heavenly realms, me just out of Eden.

Soon enough, Adam and his new wife Eve were expelled from the garden (I will let them tell you that story) and word had spread far and wide that I was the worst kind of creature. They claimed that because I was not submissive, I was not a woman, but a demon bent on killing innocent babies because I could not have my own.

The small-mindedness exhausted me. Has someone ever made an assumption about you simply because you were a boy or a girl; had blond, black or red hair; had light or dark skin?

It is maddening because none of those outside traits has a thing to do with who we are inside. The whole world decided that because I would not submit to a man's authority that I was not a "real" woman.

But I knew—and that divine spark within me confirmed—that not only was I a real woman, I carried within me God's original design for womanhood. I was the only woman alive who did, and with no children to pass it on to, I feared it would disappear when I was no longer here.

I needn't have worried. Again, God had a plan to keep my spark alive. It turns out that even though nearly every woman on Earth considered herself a daughter of Eve, there were a few who had the same strong sense of self that I did. They were not my biological daughters, but they shared my spirit.

These were the women who didn't follow the path laid before them simply because the world directed them toward it. These women listened to their inner voices. They knew God was in them and they were in God. They understood this sacred oneness, and they acted on it, despite what people thought of them.

I'll tell you a secret that has saved me many times—what other people think of us is none of our business. That's right. It only hurts us if we let it.

And so, despite the horrific rumors that paint me as a monster to this day, my spirit—the strong, independent one God planted in me so long ago—is alive in women and girls all over this world. How will you know it?

Every time you see a woman stand up to those who would rather she sit; speak out in the face of those who would prefer her silent; say no when the world tells her what she "should" do, you are seeing my legacy. You are seeing Lilith, the forgotten first woman of this world.

***

INVOCATION: Open your time together using a sound element—singing bowl, chant, drum, etc.

OPENING CIRCLE: Sit in silence for one minute, palms touching each other's.

This is not merely a formality but a way of intentionally connecting the members of the circle to one another. If this is a virtual format, adapt by sitting with palms outstretched as if you could reach out and touch your palms to the people who appear on either side of you on your screen. Even over great distances, you can create energetic connections with each other.

OPENING QUOTE:

"If the first woman God ever made was strong enough to turn the world upside down all alone, together women ought to be able to turn it rightside up again." —Sojourner Truth

EXPLORATION: WHO IS LILITH?

This is your group's jumping off point, where you establish an understanding of who Lilith was and is, in a historical, theological and cultural sense. Members of your group will likely have varying levels of familiarity with Lilith and divergent ideas about her. This session will help level the playing field and allow you all to build a foundation for the work to come.

SUGGESTED READINGS:

These pieces were chosen because they speak to the question, "Who is Lilith?" Some were written by women who know Lilith well, some by women who were recently acquainted with her.

Go around the circle, allowing all participants a chance to read, *if* they want to. Participants may read the piece in its entirety (if short) or an excerpt (if longer). The reader can select the passage(s) if excerpting. Let yourself be guided to the words your group needs to hear. Take up to five minutes to discuss each writing or piece of art.

My College Roommate by Priscilla Warner (pp. 1-3)

Painting from *The Song of Lilith* by Liliana Kleiner, Ph.D. (p. 12) IMAGE

The Song of Lilith by Liliana Kleiner, Ph.D. (pp. 14-17)

Birth Mother by Monette Chilson (pp. 9-11)

Lilith I Am by Arlene Bailey (p. 111)

The Coming of Lilith by Arlene Bailey (p. 112) IMAGE

WRITING PROMPT: *Who is Lilith?*

Write about your experience with Lilith prior to this group OR about something that resonated with you in one of today's readings.

JOURNALING TIME: 5 minutes of silence to write on the prompt. If you find you have extra time or prefer not to write, feel free to color the back coloring pages of this book or draw your answers.

CIRCLE SHARING: Optional, not mandatory; can set a time limit if desired.

CLOSING CIRCLE: Sit in silence for one minute, palms touching each other's energetically or physically as determined by each group.

BENEDICTION: *I Am Lilith* (C. Ara Campbell) p. 198

HOMEWORK:

Read *Lilith: The Essence* by Maureen Owen (pp. 27-35) before the next circle. Highlight a passage or two that particularly interests you. Members can share their highlights during next week's reading time.

Painting Lilith, Queering Lilith by Rev. Dr. Angela Yarber

Session 2: HOW HAS LILITH BEEN DISTORTED & SUPPRESSED?

GROUP TENETS:

Start by reminding your group of the environment you are creating—one that is safe, confidential and loving. One where we all get to participate at a level that is comfortable for us. No one person or person should monopolize the group's time. You may choose to remind members that we are here to support, not fix, one another. Remember, you can choose to use one of the graphics from our introduction or create your own to visually convey your group's tenets.

You can also provide logistical guidance here—silence cellphones, snack availability and restroom directions if in person; muting when not speaking, chat availability and procedures for sharing if on Zoom. I find it easier to simply have the person who wants to speak unmute and do so, though you can also suggest the hand raising function.

INTRODUCTORY READING: *Invocation of Lilith* by Nuit Moore (p. 220)

INVOCATION: Open your time together using a sound element—singing bowl, chant, drum, etc.

OPENING CIRCLE: Sit in silence for one minute, palms touching each other's.

This is not merely a formality but a way of intentionally connecting the members of the circle to one another. If this is a virtual format, adapt by sitting with palms outstretched as if you could reach out and touch your palms to the people who appear on either side of you on your screen. Even over great distances, you can create energetic connections with each other.

OPENING QUOTE:

"We must traverse the annals of history to unearth the sacred sites that have been violently gentrified by white patriarchy. We must find the Divine Truth that cannot be claimed, contained or tamed. What better place to start than at the beginning with Lilith, the world's first woman."
—Christena Cleveland, Ph.D.

EXPLORATION: HOW HAS LILITH BEEN DISTORTED & SUPPRESSED?

In our last session we looked at who Lilith is and was, through many different lenses. Now that our understanding of her is growing, let us turn our attention to how her embodied feminine power has been distorted and suppressed, while also exploring the motives for such twisting of truth. This session will serve to help us separate our truth about Lilith (and feminine strength) from the cultural and religious amalgam we have absorbed.

SUGGESTED READINGS:

Go around the circle, allowing all participants a chance to read, *if* they want to. These pieces were chosen because they speak to today's exploration, "How has Lilith been distorted and suppressed?" Participants may read the piece in its entirety (if short) or an excerpt (if longer). The reader can select the passage(s) if excerpting. Take up to five minutes to discuss each writing or piece of art.

Lilith Reviled, La Muerte Revered by Anna Keller (pp. 71-73)

The Forgotten First Woman by Arna Baartz (p. 145) IMAGE

Painting Lilith, Queering Lilith by Rev. Dr. Angela Yarber (pp. 151-153)

Painting Lilith, Queering Lilith by Rev. Dr. Angela Yarber (p. 154) IMAGE

Lilith: The Essence by Maureen Owen (pp. 27-35)

Note: have members read their highlights from the homework assignment.

WRITING PROMPT: *How has Lilith been distorted and suppressed?*

Write about ways Lilith's story has been twisted to fit certain agendas OR about something that resonated with you in one of today's readings.

JOURNALING TIME: 5 minutes of silence to write on the prompt.

CIRCLE SHARING: Optional, not mandatory; can set a time limit if desired.

CLOSING CIRCLE: Sit in silence for one minute, palms touching each other's energetically or physically as determined by each group.

BENEDICTION: *The Garden of Lilith* by C. Ara Campbell (pp. 19-21)

HOMEWORK:

Read *Lilith as Sexual Liberator* by Joey Morris (pp. 40-47) before the next circle. Highlight a passage or two that particularly interests you. Members can share their highlights during next week's reading time.

JOURNALING PAGES:

Lilith Goddess Mask by Lauren Raine

Session 3: WHAT DOES LILITH STIR OR REAWAKEN IN YOU?

GROUP TENETS:

This is where you remind your group of the environment you are creating—one that is safe, confidential and loving. One where we all get to participate at a level that is comfortable for us. No one person or person should monopolize the group's time. You may choose to remind members that we are here to support, not fix, one another. Remember, you can choose to use one of the graphics from our introduction or create your own to visually convey your group's tenets.

You can also provide logistical guidance here—silence cellphones, snack availability and restroom directions if in person; muting when not speaking, chat availability and procedures for sharing if on Zoom. I find it easier to simply have the person who wants to speak unmute and do so, though you can also suggest the hand raising function.

INTRODUCTORY READING: *Clay, not bone* by Donna Snyder (p. 26)

INVOCATION: Open your time together using a sound element—singing bowl, chant, drum, etc.

OPENING CIRCLE: Sit in silence for one minute, palms touching each other's.

This is not merely a formality but a way of intentionally connecting the members of the circle to one another. If this is a virtual format, adapt by sitting with palms outstretched as if you could reach out and touch your palms to the people who appear on either side of you on your screen. Even over great distances, you can create energetic connections with each other.

OPENING QUOTE:

"Lilith is our sacred sovereignty. And so thus, Her mythos has been subject to those forces that would tame the primal female. Many of the "his-stories" of Lilith have the same rotten core of fear and domination—of the attempted subjugation of Her." —Nuit Moore

EXPLORATION: WHAT DOES LILITH STIR OR REAWAKEN IN YOU?

In this third session, we conclude Part One of our study by turning our discovery of Lilith inward. Last session we looked at how Lilith's embodied feminine power has been distorted and suppressed. This week we will explore how our discovery of Lilith's archetypal female strength is affecting us. Reflect on what is rising to the surface for you.

SUGGESTED READINGS:

Go around the circle, allowing all participants a chance to read, *if* they want to. These pieces were chosen because they speak to the question, "What does Lilith stir or reawaken in you?" Participants may read the piece in its entirety (if short) or an excerpt (if longer). The reader can select the passage(s) if excerpting. If technology permits, you may also project the image on a screen, making sure you credit the artist. Take up to five minutes to discuss each writing or piece of art.

At Last I Grew Wings by Lauren Raine (pp. 75-76)

Lilith Goddess Mask by Lauren Raine (p. 74) IMAGE

Ode to a Sudanese Girl by Joyce McCauley-Benner (p. 144)

The Deep Within by Lucy Pierce (p. 121) IMAGE

Lilith's Song (*Fly Away*) by Vicki Scotti (p. 150)

Lilith as Sexual Liberator by Joey Morris (pp. 40-47)

Note: have members read their highlights from the homework assignment.

WRITING PROMPT: *What does Lilith stir or reawaken in you?*

Write about what Lilith's story is stirring within you. There is no right or wrong answer. If you are still processing your inner awakenings, you may also choose to write about something that resonated with you in one of today's readings, as a way of deepening your own integration.

JOURNALING TIME: 5 minutes of silence to write on the prompt.

CIRCLE SHARING: Optional, not mandatory; can set a time limit if desired.

CLOSING CIRCLE: Sit in silence for one minute, palms touching each other's energetically or physically as determined by each group.

BENEDICTION: *Outraged Ancestral Mother Prayer* by Molly Remer (pp. 205-206)

HOMEWORK:

Read *Daughters of Lilith Can Be Muslim Too* by Riem Farahat (p. 50-56). Please read this before the next circle. Highlight a passage or two that particularly interests you. Members can share their highlights during next week's reading time.

JOURNALING PAGES:

PART 2—RECLAIMING LILITH

All our lives, we have been given one overarching myth about the origins of feminine nature. That tale involves a paradise and a woman who eats an apple and ruins it all. The story goes that she can't be trusted and that her femaleness is the reason. Her female nature makes her susceptible and easily tricked. Unfit to lead lest she succumb to her inherent moral weakness.

In this version of the story, she is to subdue her nature—because it leads to dangerous things. She is to be submissive to males and to the male way. And this story has been sanctified as unquestionable religious doctrine that formed the bedrock of patriarchy.

My sisters, it is time to question.

It is time to lean into different stories and different archetypes of feminine origin. It is time to listen for our foremothers' voices as they tell us their story.

If we believe patriarchal stories about our origins, we will become the women the patriarchy needs to sustain it.

If we write new stories, we become women who cannot be constrained by patriarchy.

In this re-writing of the female story, we will delve into what Lilith teaches us about feminine strength that patriarchal myths have not (session four); we will look at the resistance we might have to discarding the deeply ingrained myth of Eve and explore how Eve might be viewed if the lens of patriarchy were removed (session five); and we will sit and listen to how this all affects our self-image and the image of our creator (session six).

Painting by Arna Baartz – Cover Art for *Original Resistance*

Session 4: WHAT DOES LILITH TEACH US ABOUT FEMININE STRENGTH?

GROUP TENETS:

This is where you remind your group of the environment you are creating—one that is safe, confidential and loving. One where we all get to participate at a level that is comfortable for us. No one person or person should monopolize the group's time. You may choose to remind members that we are here to support, not fix, one another. Remember, you can choose to use one of the graphics from our introduction or create your own to visually convey your group's tenets.

You can also provide logistical guidance here—silence cellphones, snack availability and restroom directions if in person; muting when not speaking, chat availability and procedures for sharing if on Zoom. I find it easier to simply have the person who wants to speak unmute and do so, though you can also suggest the hand raising function.

INTRODUCTORY READING: *Hymn to Lilith* by Nuit Moore (p. 84)

INVOCATION: Open your time together using a sound element—singing bowl, chant, drum, etc.

OPENING CIRCLE: Sit in silence for one minute, palms touching each other's.

This is not merely a formality but a way of intentionally connecting the members of the circle to one another. If this is a virtual format, adapt by sitting with palms outstretched as if you could reach out and touch your palms to the people who appear on either side of you on your screen. Even over great distances, you can create energetic connections with each other.

OPENING QUOTE:

"Do what you feel in your heart to be right, for you'll be criticized anyway." —Eleanor Roosevelt

EXPLORATION: WHAT DOES LILITH TEACH US ABOUT FEMININE STRENGTH?

Strength has been masculinized and its masculinization internalized by men and women. A masculinized version of strength focuses on physical prowess, specifically on who can do the most—lift the most, throw the farthest, hit the hardest. What if we reimagined our conceptualization of strength? What if the lifting, throwing and hitting that matter are lifting ourselves and others up, throwing away toxicity and hitting the ground firmly with our feet each morning, grateful to walk through the day ahead?

SUGGESTED READINGS:

Note: While you listen today, write down words that jump out to you. Don't think too hard or try to figure out why they caught your attention. Just jot them down and return to listening. Take up to five minutes to discuss each writing or piece of art.

No Turning Back by Birgit Langhammer (pp. 38-39)

Goddess #5 by Birgit Langhammer (p. 37) IMAGE

Hear Lilith by Patricia Campagna (pp. 48-49)

Lilith Rising by Arlene Bailey (p. 116) IMAGE

Lilith—Sacred Sovereignty of the Womanspirit by Nuit Moore (pp. 146-149)

Daughters of Lilith Can Be Muslim Too by Riem Farahat (pp. 50-56)

Note: have members read their highlights from the homework assignment.

WRITING PROMPT: *What does Lilith teach us about feminine strength?*

Let's reimagine what strength means to us. Review the words that caught your attention in the readings. Do any of these words convey your evolving ideas about strength? Does Lilith embody any of your strength words? Write your own definition of strength.

JOURNALING TIME: 5 minutes of silence to write on the prompt.

CIRCLE SHARING: Optional, not mandatory; can set a time limit if desired.

CLOSING CIRCLE: Sit in silence for one minute, palms touching each other's energetically or physically as determined by each group.

BENEDICTION: *Ode to Lilith* by Joyce McCauley-Benner (p. 143)

HOMEWORK:

Read *Lilith & Eve* by Luisah Teish (pp. 133-142) before the next circle. Highlight a passage or two that particularly interests you. Members can share their highlights during next week's reading time.

Garden of Eden by Asia Morgenthaler

Session 5: DO I HAVE TO CHOOSE BETWEEN LILITH & EVE?

GROUP TENETS:

This is where you remind your group of the environment you are creating—one that is safe, confidential and loving. One where we all get to participate at a level that is comfortable for us. No one person or person should monopolize the group's time. You may choose to remind members that we are here to support, not fix, one another. Remember, you can choose to use one of the graphics from our introduction or create your own to visually convey your group's tenets.

You can also provide logistical guidance here—silence cellphones, snack availability and restroom directions if in person; muting when not speaking, chat availability and procedures for sharing if on Zoom. I find it easier to simply have the person who wants to speak unmute and do so, though you can also suggest the hand raising function.

INTRODUCTORY READING: *Lilith Eve, a Child and a Woman for our Tomorrows* by Lizette Galima Tapia-Raquel (pp. 88-89)

INVOCATION: Open your time together using a sound element—singing bowl, chant, drum, etc.

OPENING CIRCLE: Sit in silence for one minute, palms touching each other's.

This is not merely a formality but a way of intentionally connecting the members of the circle to one another. If this is a virtual format, adapt by sitting with palms outstretched as if you could reach out and touch your palms to the people who appear on either side of you on your screen. Even over great distances, you can create energetic connections with each other.

OPENING QUOTE:

"Female resistance is dangerous. It is also necessary. For far too long the Western Judeo-Christian stigma of Eve as the downfall of humankind has served to oppress women, silence our voices, desecrate our power, annihilate our very existence. As an archetype of female strength and sovereignty, Lilith is the missing link in our spiritual mitochondria. Inviolable. Self-defining. Autonomous. She reminds us that we can, and must, resist any and all attempts to silence our voices, diminish our strength, erase our lived-experience. Original Resistance: Reclaiming Lilith, Reclaiming Ourselves is a veritable feast of artwork, poetry, and prose by visual artists and writers from a wide range of ethnicities, cultures, and countries around the world. It nourishes the soul and inspires us to embrace the wild beauty of our nature, and dance with abandon. Ultimately, it urges us to remember and reclaim our right—our duty—to resist all attempts to oppress and subvert our innate power. Like Lilith, it calls us to denounce the patriarchally-enforced feminine role of subservience, and restore our rightful place in the world." —Mary Saracino

EXPLORATION: DO I HAVE TO CHOOSE BETWEEN LILITH & EVE?

In this fifth session, we continue venturing into Part Two of our study—Reclaiming Lilith—allowing ourselves to look critically at the two primary "first female" paradigms in Western society. After embracing Lilith as teacher in our last session, we look at Lilith and Eve—presented as competing paradigms of femininity—and begin to interpret them for ourselves.

SUGGESTED READINGS:

Go around the circle, allowing all participants a chance to read, *if* they want to. These pieces were chosen because they speak to the feminine archetypal conundrum, "Do we have to choose between Lilith and Eve?" Participants may read the piece in its entirety (if short) or an excerpt (if longer). The reader can select the passage(s) if excerpting. If time/resources exist, you may also project the selected image on a screen, making sure you credit the artist. Take up to five minutes to discuss each writing or piece of art.

Eve by Lucy Pierce (pp. 102-105)

Painting from *The Song of Lilith* by Liliana Kleiner, Ph.D. (p. 18) IMAGE

Daughter of Lilith by Tamara Albanna (pp. 99-100)

Garden of Eden by Asia Morgenthaler (p. 57) IMAGE

Lilith & Eve by Luisah Teish (pp. 133-142)

Note: have members read their highlights from the homework assignment.

WRITING PROMPT: *Do I have to choose between Lilith and Eve?*

Let's be clear that these stories are myths—stories that exist to carry deeper truths to us. They are not fact-based narratives that can or should be proven factually correct or incorrect. They are neither right nor wrong, for they exceed the limits of such dualistic parameters. With that in mind, you are not required to choose an archetype. You are free to sit with both Lilith and Eve. To meditate on their stories. In today's writing time, question how their stories have been told and to re-write narratives to align with your inner truth. For that, sisters, is the truth that matters.

JOURNALING TIME: 5 minutes of silence to write on the prompt.

CIRCLE SHARING: Optional, not mandatory; can set a time limit if desired.

CLOSING CIRCLE: Sit in silence for one minute, palms touching each other's energetically or physically as determined by each group.

BENEDICTION:

"The Genesis myth is a myth in a world of myths. It is not the myth of the world. More likely, it is the story of a culture imposing itself upon another with dire consequences for Woman, her self-image and her place in the culture." —Luisah Teish, excerpted from our homework, *Lilith & Eve* (p. 138)

HOMEWORK:

Read *The Dark Goddess in the Sky* by Nicole Fair (pp. 106-110 before the next circle. Highlight a passage or two that particularly interests you. Members can share their highlights during next week's reading time.

Session 6: How does Lilith's story affect my self-image and my creator image?

GROUP TENETS:

This is where you remind your group of the environment you are creating—one that is safe, confidential and loving. One where we all get to participate at a level that is comfortable for us. No one person or person should monopolize the group's time. You may choose to remind members that we are here to support, not fix, one another. Remember, you can choose to use one of the graphics from our introduction or create your own to visually convey your group's tenets.

You can also provide logistical guidance here—silence cellphones, snack availability and restroom directions if in person; muting when not speaking, chat availability and procedures for sharing if on Zoom. I find it easier to simply have the person who wants to speak unmute and do so, though you can also suggest the hand raising function.

OPENING QUOTES:

"In the beginning people prayed to the Creatures of Life. At the very dawn of religion, God was a woman." —Merlin Stone

"For I am the earth from which the garden blooms and she, my mother, carries me on Her back in every living moment. She will not have me forget who it is that I am. How deeply I belong in the matrix of Her love. I have come home to the garden, and it is in need of my tending, for the eons have swelled in the wake of my forgetting, upon the false tides of the myth that I am separate." —Lucy Pierce

INTRODUCTORY READING:

Reclaiming Our Time: Why Women Must Uncover Our Ancient History by Christena Cleveland., Ph.D. (pp. 5-8)

INVOCATION: Open your time together using a sound element—singing bowl, chant, drum, etc.

OPENING CIRCLE: Sit in silence for one minute, palms touching each other's.

This is not merely a formality but a way of intentionally connecting the members of the circle to one another. If this is a virtual format, adapt by sitting with palms outstretched as if you could reach out and touch your palms to the people who appear on either side of you on your screen. Even over great distances, you can create energetic connections with each other.

EXPLORATION: HOW DOES LILITH'S STORY AFFECT MY SELF & CREATOR IMAGES?

Our work together will be merely interesting, rather than transformative, if we do not allow it to penetrate to our core identities of self and divinity. The stories we tell ourselves about who we are and who our creator is matter. Mine began shifting after I integrated a different creation myth. Perhaps yours will too.

SUGGESTED READINGS:

These pieces were chosen because they paint a poetic picture of a reimagined vision of the female self and our relationship to the divine. Participants may read the piece in its entirety (if short) or an excerpt (if longer). The reader can select the passage(s) if excerpting. If time and resources exist, you may also project the selected image on a screen, making sure you credit the artist. Take up to five minutes to discuss each writing or piece of art.

Lilith and the Black Madonna by Susan Scott (pp. 188-190)

Lilith Stained Glass Window by Breanna Bowling (p. 83) IMAGE

The Hag's Prayer, Hissed from Crone to Innocent by Danielle Dulsky (pp. 199-200)

Wind Dancer Wind by Elisabeth Slettnes (p. 207) IMAGE

The Dark Goddess in the Sky by Nicole Fair (pp. 106-110)

Note: have members read their highlights from the homework assignment.

WRITING PROMPT: *How does Lilith's story affect my self and creator images?*

Our reimagining of the creation story and its implications for female identity has led us to a place where we can begin to reimagine ourselves and our conception of divinity. Write about how Lilith's story has impacted those two key identities for you.

JOURNALING TIME: 5 minutes of silence to write on the prompt.

CIRCLE SHARING: Optional, not mandatory; can set a time limit if desired.

CLOSING CIRCLE: Sit in silence for one minute, palms touching each other's energetically or physically as determined by each group.

BENEDICTION: *Shamelessly Naked* by Donna Snyder (p. 132)

HOMEWORK:

Read *Lessons from the Dark Mother* by Jaclyn Cherie (pp. 125-131) before the next circle. Highlight a passage or two that particularly interests you. Members can share their highlights during next week's reading time.

PART THREE—RECLAIMING OURSELVES

Now we synthesize. We know there were stories about our origins that were hidden from us. We know Lilith was one of those stories. In her, we have recognized parts of ourselves that didn't fit our old molds of femininity. We have redefined both femininity and strength through this new lens. Our view of our creator and of ourselves have begun to shift.

It is time to reclaim ourselves in light of all this new knowing.

In this self-reclamation, we will own the parts of ourselves that we'd exiled as unfeminine (session seven); we will identify Lilith's traits that we want to incorporate into our own way of being; we will acknowledge that Lilith's brand of femininity is just as viable as other more traditionally feminine models (session eight); and, finally we will sit and listen to how we can embody this in our own lives now (session nine).

In the back of this workbook, you will find some bonus coloring pages. Reclaim some of your time for play and color outside the lines! You can also draw how you envision Lilith. There will be time at the last circle to share for those who want to.

The Wound by Lucy Pierce

Session 7: Can we embrace our "unfeminine" parts?

GROUP TENETS:

This is where you remind your group of the environment you are creating—one that is safe, confidential and loving. One where we all get to participate at a level that is comfortable for us. No one person or person should monopolize the group's time. You may choose to remind members that we are here to support, not fix, one another. Remember, you can choose to use one of the graphics from our introduction or create your own to visually convey your group's tenets.

You can also provide logistical guidance here—silence cellphones, snack availability and restroom directions if in person; muting when not speaking, chat availability and procedures for sharing if on Zoom. I find it easier to simply have the person who wants to speak unmute and do so, though you can also suggest the hand raising function.

OPENING QUOTE:

"They asked her 'how did you free yourself?' She answered, 'by embracing my own power."
—Yung Pueblo

INTRODUCTORY READING:

The Outraged Ancestral Mother by Molly Remer (pp. 202-204)

INVOCATION: Open your time together using a sound element—singing bowl, chant, drum, etc.

OPENING CIRCLE: Sit in silence for one minute, palms touching each other's.

This is not merely a formality but a way of intentionally connecting the members of the circle to one another. If this is a virtual format, adapt by sitting with palms outstretched as if you could reach out and touch your palms to the people who appear on either side of you on your screen. Even over great distances, you can create energetic connections with each other.

EXPLORATION: CAN WE EMBRACE OUR "UNFEMININE" PARTS?

In this session, our work is part dismantling, part redefining and part integration. This is roughly analogous to the recovery work of awareness, acceptance and action. We must see the parts of us that we have suppressed or denied (awareness). We must accept our newly evolving definition of what it means to be feminine (acceptance). And, finally, we must integrate this new definition into the way we move through the world (action).

SUGGESTED READINGS:

Go around the circle, allowing all participants a chance to read, *if* they want to. These pieces were chosen because they speak to the false assumption that certain characteristics are accepted as feminine while others aren't. They are included because the challenge our indoctrination about what it means to be feminine. They are here to shake and awaken us.

Participants may read the piece in its entirety (if short) or an excerpt (if longer). The reader can select the passage(s) if excerpting. If time/resources exist, you may also project the selected image on a screen, making sure you credit the artist. Take up to five minutes to discuss each writing or piece of art.

Reclaim Lilith and BE the Original Resistance by Hazel DeHealer (pp. 85-86)

The Wound by Lucy Pierce (p. 101) IMAGE

Lilith Speaks by Molly Remer (p. 98)

The Song of Lilith II by Liliana Kleiner, Ph.D. (p. 183) IMAGE

Lessons from the Dark Mother by Jaclyn Cherie (pp. 125-131)

Note: have members read their highlights from the homework assignment.

WRITING PROMPT: *How can we embrace our "unfeminine parts?"*

Follow the model of awareness, acceptance and action described in the exploration section. Write about your awareness of the parts of you that you have rejected as unfeminine; your acceptance of a new definition of femininity; and the action you will take as a result of that new definition.

JOURNALING TIME: 5 minutes of silence to write on the prompt.

CIRCLE SHARING: Optional, not mandatory; can set a time limit if desired.

CLOSING CIRCLE: Sit in silence for one minute, palms touching each other's energetically or physically as determined by each group.

BENEDICTION: *Ashes and Spark* by K.A. Laity (p. 22)

HOMEWORK:

Read *The First Resister: Evoking Lilith for Transformation and Freedom* by D'vorah J. Grenn, Ph.D. (by pp. 60-67 before the next circle. Highlight a passage or two that particularly interests you. Members can share their highlights during next week's reading time.

Lilith Stained Glass Window by Breanna Bowling

Session 8: What does Lilith model that I desire?

GROUP TENETS:

This is where you remind your group of the environment you are creating—one that is safe, confidential and loving. One where we all get to participate at a level that is comfortable for us. No one person or person should monopolize the group's time. You may choose to remind members that we are here to support, not fix, one another. Remember, you can choose to use one of the graphics from our introduction or create your own to visually convey your group's tenets.

You can also provide logistical guidance here—silence cellphones, snack availability and restroom directions if in person; muting when not speaking, chat availability and procedures for sharing if on Zoom. I find it easier to simply have the person who wants to speak unmute and do so, though you can also suggest the hand raising function.

OPENING QUOTE:

"Lilith is the Goddess of women who do not settle. She is the essence of the wild woman spirit."
—Nuit Moore

INTRODUCTORY READING:

And I Rise by Arlene Bailey (p. 117)

INVOCATION: Open your time together using a sound element—singing bowl, chant, drum, etc.

OPENING CIRCLE: Sit in silence for one minute, palms touching each other's.

This is not merely a formality but a way of intentionally connecting the members of the circle to one another. If this is a virtual format, adapt by sitting with palms outstretched as if you could reach out and touch your palms to the people who appear on either side of you on your screen. Even over great distances, you can create energetic connections with each other.

EXPLORATION: WHAT DOES LILITH MODEL THAT I DESIRE?

No one archetype will embody all part of your unique femininity. You may have maternal instincts or a softer side that are mirrored more clearly for you in other archetypes. Lilith's brand of femininity, however, has been left out of the version of womanhood we've been offered. This is your opportunity to mine the richness of these not-so-typical womanly ways. Do you want more irreverence in your life? Perhaps a bit of devil-may-care attitude? Do you wish you were less of a rule follower? Do you dare to cultivate more independence?

SUGGESTED READINGS:

These pieces were chosen because they highlight different aspects of Lilith, fleshing out the archetype so that we can harness her power for growth in our own lives. As the pieces are read, listen for words that feel like they are calling you. These may be the very traits you would like to borrow from Lilith.

Participants may read the piece in its entirety (if short) or an excerpt (if longer). The reader can select the passage(s) if excerpting. If time/resources exist, you may also project the selected image on a screen, making sure you credit the artist. Take up to five minutes to discuss each writing or piece of art.

Lilith Rising by Arlene Bailey (p. 116) IMAGE

And I Rise by Arlene Bailey (p. 117)

Joyous Lilith by Nuit Moore (p. 219) IMAGE

Anointing the Lilith Within by Rita Lucey (p. 185-186)

The First Resister: Evoking Lilith for Transformation and Freedom by D'vorah J. Grenn, Ph.D. (pp. 60-67)

Note: have members read their highlights from the homework assignment.

WRITING PROMPT: *What does Lilith model that I desire?*

Look over the words you wrote down from the readings. Circle the ones that describe parts of Lilith you want to embody. Write about why you want these traits in your life.

JOURNALING TIME: 5 minutes of silence to write on the prompt.

CIRCLE SHARING: Optional, not mandatory; can set a time limit if desired.

CLOSING CIRCLE: Sit in silence for one minute, palms touching each other's energetically or physically as determined by each group.

BENEDICTION: *Lessons from Lilith* by Paige Nolan (p. 191-192)

HOMEWORK:

Read *The Status Quo Has to Go* by Trista Hendren (p. 208-218) before the next circle. Highlight a passage or two that particularly interests you. Members can share their highlights during next week's reading time. Please also take some time to review your journal and the highlighted passages in your anthology. Decide if there is anything you would like to share with the group during our final circle. If you have not done the coloring pages yet, you may want to set aside some time to do so.

Joyous Lilith by Nuit Moore

Session 9: What action does Lilith inspire in me?

GROUP TENETS:

This is where you remind your group of the environment you are creating—one that is safe, confidential and loving. One where we all get to participate at a level that is comfortable for us. No one person or person should monopolize the group's time. You may choose to remind members that we are here to support, not fix, one another. Remember, you can choose to use one of the graphics from our introduction or create your own to visually convey your group's tenets.

You can also provide logistical guidance here—silence cellphones, snack availability and restroom directions if in person; muting when not speaking, chat availability and procedures for sharing if on Zoom. I find it easier to simply have the person who wants to speak unmute and do so, though you can also suggest the hand raising function.

OPENING QUOTE: "Those who do not move do not notice their chains." —Rosa Luxemburg

INTRODUCTORY READING: *Another Way* by Monette Chilson (p. 69-70)

INVOCATION: Open your time together using a sound element—singing bowl, chant, drum, etc.

OPENING CIRCLE: Sit in silence for one minute, palms touching each other's.

This is not merely a formality but a way of intentionally connecting the members of the circle to one another. If this is a virtual format, adapt by sitting with palms outstretched as if you could reach out and touch your palms to the people who appear on either side of you on your screen. Even over great distances, you can create energetic connections with each other.

EXPLORATION: WHAT ACTION DOES LILITH INSPIRE IN ME?

This session will launch you into your Lilith consciousness. Trust that by this point, you know what you need to know and you have processed what you need to process. You are fully equipped to live a life of sovereignty. To be the boss of your own damn self! Use this last session together to motivate each other to go forth as newly awakened daughters of Lilith.

SUGGESTED READINGS:

Go around the circle, allowing all participants a chance to read, *if* they want to. These pieces were chosen because they are all manifestos of sort—some declaring female sovereignty and some highlighting it through narrative or imagery.

Participants may read the piece in its entirety (if short) or an excerpt (if longer). The reader can select the passage(s) if excerpting. For visual art, you may share the image (via screen share or projection), making sure to credit the artist. Take up to five minutes to discuss each writing or piece of art.

She Meets Herself by Lucy Pierce (p. 87) IMAGE

Lilith as Archetypal Guide by Lauren Raine (pp. 193-197)

My Body, Her Body by Arlene Bailey (pp. 113-115)

Transforming Vision by Elisabeth Slettnes (p. 222) IMAGE

The Status Quo Has to Go by Trista Hendren (p. 208-218)

Note: have members read their highlights from the homework assignment. This is also the time to share anything particularly meaningful from the anthology, time in circle or journal insights. You may also want to take some time to share your Coloring pages at the end of the workbook. Make sure that each woman has time to share for 3-5 minutes if she would like to.

WRITING PROMPT: *What action does Lilith inspire in me?*

This is the last prompt of our work together in this Lilith Circle, and it is meant as a jumping off point. A great journey starts with just one step, and that is exactly where we will leave each other, stepping onto our paths. Write about this very first step—one specific action Lilith is prompting you to take. It can sound small. Perhaps it is small. But it is the beginning of something that can fundamentally change the way you show up in this one precious life of yours.

JOURNALING TIME: 5 minutes of silence to write on the prompt.

CIRCLE SHARING: Optional, not mandatory; can set a time limit if desired.

CALL TO CONSCIOUSNESS:

"As our literal oceans swell with and our world reverberates with racism and male violence, we must embrace Lilith's massive energy. I call on Lilith to guide us out of this man-made mess that patriarchy has piled onto for thousands of years. The status quo is no longer acceptable. I re-commit my life to doing whatever it takes to overturn it. I ask you to join me." —Trista Hendren, *The Status Quo Has to Go* by Trista Hendren (pp. 208-218)

CLOSING CIRCLE: Sit in silence for one minute, palms touching each other's energetically or physically as determined by each group.

BENEDICTION: *Reclaiming Ourselves* by Trista Hendren (p. 223-224)

HOMEWORK:

Take some extra time to journal and think about what you have learned through this course and your circle sisters. Go back through and read your previous entries and highlighted passages in *Original Resistance.*

Further Exploration: A Lilith Resource List

NON-FICTION

A God Who Looks Like Me (Patricia Lynn Reilly)

A Song of Lilith (Joy Kogawa; illustrated by Lilian Broca)

Dark Goddess Magick – Rituals and Spells for Reclaiming your Feminine Fire (C. Ara Campbell)

Embracing Lilith (Mark H. Williams)

Goddess Reclaimed: 13 Initiations to Unleash Your Sacred Feminine Power (Syma Kharal)

In Praise of Lilith, Eve & The Serpent in the Garden of Eden & Other Stories (Susan Scott)

Lilith—The First Eve (Siegmund Hurtwitz)

Lilith: The Legend of the First Woman (Ada Langworthy Collier)

Lilith's Fire—Reclaiming Our Sacred Life-Force (D'vorah Grenn)

The Book of Lilith (Barbara Black Koltuv)

The Book of Lilith (Robert G. Brown)

The Coming of Lilith: Essays on Feminism, Judaism & Sexual Ethics (Judith Plaskow)

The Hebrew Goddess (Rafael Patai)

The Song of Lilith (Liliana Kleiner, with illustrations by Liliana Kleiner as well.)

LITERARY CRITICISM

Lilith's Daughters: Women & Religion in Contemporary Fiction (Barbara Hill Rigney)

Mythmaking & Metaphor in Black Women's Fiction (Jacqueline de Weever)

ANTHOLOGIES

Lilith: Dark Feminine Archetype (Asenath Mason)

Original Resistance: Reclaiming Lilith, Reclaiming Ourselves (Monette Chilson)

WomanSpirit Rising: A Feminist Reader in Religion (Carol P. Christ & Judith Plaskow)

FICTION

Heroes and Villians (Angela Carter)

Sula (Toni Morrison)

The Passion of New Eve (Angela Carter)

The Sadeian Woman (Angela Carter)

POETRY

Of Lilith and Delilah (M ^ h)

WEBSITES

The Lilith Institute (www.LilithInstitute.com)

FOR CHILDREN

My Name is Lilith (Monette Chilson; illustrated by Arna Baartz)

Thank you for joining us on this journey! Stay tuned for future anthologies
and Circle Guides.

***

BONUS: Lilith Coloring Pages can be found on the next pages!

The first 4 were early sketches for *My Name is Lilith*, illustrated by Arna Baartz.

The last one is *Joyous Lilith* by Nuit Moore.

***

If you have enjoyed this book, please write a brief review on Amazon and/or Goodreads!

Find more books at:
www.thegirlgod.com

Joyous Lilith
NightMoore '04